The Critter from Another Litter

Heidi Mitchell

Illustrated by Carmen Newell

Copyright © 2025 Heidi Mitchell

All rights reserved.

No part of this book may be reproduced, stored in a retrieval system,
or transmitted by any means, electronic, mechanical, photocopying, recording,
or otherwise, without written permission from the author.

ISBN (Paperback): 979-8-9919700-0-6
ISBN (eBook): 979-8-9917098-9-7

The Critter from Another Litter

My sense of smell is very strong
I've known you were coming all along.
I can smell things humans might miss,
some smell like that;

There have been new things around our home.
I saw a new brush;
I saw a new comb.

Soft fluffy blankets on a bed,
toys to play with, books to be read.

New sounds and
noises fill the air.
Good sounds of laughter,
sounds of care.
Your voice saying you
want some food.
Soft nighttime music
for a sleepy mood.

Gently touching your soft warm skin.
My tail wags lightly again and again.
We snuggle together a blanket for two.
This part for me, the rest is for you.

Let's share the snack you have on your tray.
Be sure to be quick before they take it away.

Keeping you safe is a new job for me.
I'll stay right beside you diligently.
Our family is better because you are here.
Please know I will love you year after
year after year.

This book belongs to

_____

and

_____

www.ingramcontent.com/pod-product-compliance
Lightning Source LLC
LaVergne TN
LVHW070525070526
838199LV00072B/6702